APRIL: THE MONTH OF

RAPID

PROGRESS

MUKARO MATUHWA

APRIL:
MONTH OF RAPID PROGRESS
(1 Timothy 4:15)

A Gift To

....

From
Mukaro Matuhwa

....

APRIL EDITION

Declaration

I **Mukaro Matuhwa** declare that the contents of this book are all mine & none was plagiarized nor copied from anyone or any devotion organization except where I've quoted from the original source (Bible). Many thanks are due to our Lord Jesus Christ for the unmatched wisdom & rare inspiration contained herein. Feel free to allow the Holy Spirit to speak to you on how to level mountains in your endeavors as you will be reading each & every daily devotion. Thank you for being part of the readership. *Signature:*.......................

APRIL EDITION

Copyright

RAPID PROGRESS

First Edition: 01 April 2024

Book Cover Design: CMP Designers

Editing & Proof Reading: CMP Editors

Book Cover Art: CMP Designers

Interior Design: CM Publishers

Book Publisher © CMP

APRIL EDITION

Table of Contents

Contents

(1 Peter 2:1-3)

Theme: Living A Life Worthy of The Lord

(Colossians 1:10)

Theme: Growing Roots

(Colossians 2:7)

Theme: Enlarging Tents

(Isaiah 54:2-3)

Theme: Press On

(Philippians 3:13-14)

Theme: Love Abound

(Philippians 1:9-11)

Theme: Bearing Much Fruit

(John 15:5)

Theme: Character & Hope

(Romans 5:3-5)

Theme: The Aliveness of The Word of God

(Hebrews 4:12)

Theme: Mind Renewal

(Romans 12:2)

Theme: Chosen From The Beginning

(2 Thessalonians 2:13)

Theme: Are You Ready?

(1 Corinthians 3:1-3)

Theme: Go For Maturity

(Ephesians 4:13-15)

Theme: Perseverance

(Luke 8:14-15)

Theme: Mustard Seed

(Matthew 13:31-32)

Theme: Test Yourself

(2 Corinthians 13:5-7)

Theme: Abound In Thanksgiving

(Colossians 2:6-7)

Theme: Ask The Lord

(Luke 17:5)

Theme: Being Planted In The Lord's House

(Psalm 92:12-14)

Theme: Mastering Your Strengths

(Psalm 84:7)

Theme: A Sound Mind

(2 Timothy 1:7)

Theme: Being Doers of The Word of God

(James 1:22)

Theme: The Power To Get Wealth

(Deuteronomy 8:18)

Theme: Taking Delight In The Lord

(Psalm 37:4)

Victory Prayer
Salvation Call
Contact Details

Author's Desk

S eason greetings my dear Reader! I hope to find you well, fit & safe. I found it good if not the best thing to compile these teachings about rapid progress for you to start to move in paradoxes (unimaginable & unexplainable realms) of progress. So, basing on 1 Tinothy 4:15 as this month's theme verse, I've written these teachings in a progressive way such that any believer who is eager to live a better lifestyle in this new month of April can easily follow for his or her own beneficiation. Progress is bound to be evident the moment you are to start applying progress-based principles. Applied principles gives birth to undeniable progress evidence in everything that concerns you; be it social life, business life, ministry, finances, health etc. Be ready to embrace a shift in your life as you'll be going through the pages of this devotional booklet in this month of April which has been declared - month of Rapid Progress.

APRIL EDITION

Theme: Be Diligent
(1 Timothy 4:15)

1ˢᵗ Day

"Be diligent in these matters; give yourself wholly to them, so that everyone may see your progress."

B PROGRESS CONFESSION:
I'm going to be diligent in my career, business, calling & ministry! I'm going to be willing and be obedient to the Word of God for my progress' sake in Jesus'
e

diligent & give yourself wholly to anything (project) God has given you. Ecclesiastes 9:10 says & I quote, *"Whatsoever thy hand findeth to do, do it with thy might; for there is no work, nor device, nor knowledge, nor wisdom, in the grave, whither thou goest."* Whatsoever you want to see progressing well into your life, do it with might & in a wholehearted manner! Proverbs 10:4 says & I quote, *"He becometh poor that dealeth with a slack hand: but the hand of the diligent maketh rich."* It is the hand of someone who is diligent that has the capacity to make one rich. A diligent person actually understands that the power & strength to get wealth & riches comes from the Lord. Deuteronomy 8:18 says & I quote, *"But thou shalt remember the Lord thy*

God: for it is he that giveth thee power to get wealth, that he may establish his covenant which He sware unto thy fathers, as it is this day." Philippians 4:13 says & I quote, *"I can do all things through Christ which strengtheneth me."* Proverbs 10:22 says & I quote, *"The blessing of the Lord, it maketh rich & He addeth no sorrow with it."* Be diligent for the blessing of the Lord is upon you! Master your craft (trade) till you become an expert! Perfect (polish up) your works! It's better for you not to do that work if you are not going to do it wholly! A not-done at all work is better than a half-done job claimed to be fully-done! Isaiah 1:19 says & I quote, *"If ye be willing & obedient, ye shall eat the good of the land."* Just be willing & obedient to the Word of God & let's see if things are not going to change for your good. I pray for you that through your diligence display towards your career, calling, ministry, business etc. your progress is going to be mapped & noticed! It is done!

APRIL EDITION

Theme: Taking The Full Responsibility
(1 Corinthians 13:11)

2nd Day

*"When I was a child, I talked like a child, I thought like a child,
I reasoned like a child. When I became a man, I put the ways
of childhood behind me."*

> ## PROGRESS CONFESSION:
> *I take full responsibility of everything that is going to
> happen in my life! No more blame game! I'm wise!
> I'm full of God's Word (knowledgeable)!*

For your progress to be well noticed, you are advised to put aside all the childish ways & start to take full responsibility of each & everything that will be happening in your life. Start to think & reason like a responsible man, woman, brother, sister, business guru, minister, believer etc! The Lord is saying to you that come & let us reason together now (Isaiah 1:18). Revelation 3:20 says & I quote, *"Behold, I stand at the door & knock: if any man hears my voice & open the door, I will come in to him & will sup with him & he with me."* The Lord is standing at your door & knocking today, it's up to you for you to hear the knock on the door or the voice of the one knocking. Allow the Lord to come in & dine with you! It is out of you dining with him that maturity & great advises are dished out to you! Jeremiah 33:3 says & I quote, *"Call unto me & I'll answer thee & show thee great & mighty things, which thou knowest not."* Now that you have called Him & He is now on your door knocking, watch out to be shown great & might things which you have never seen before! Watch out for the unlocking of new levels in business (career) & new heights in your social life (marriage & relationships)! I prophesy that in the name of Jesus Christ, your life will never be the same again after you have dined with Him! The Lord is going to strategically position you in all spheres of life that matters! Psalm 23:2-3 says & I quote, *"He maketh me to lie down in green pastures: he leadeth me beside the still waters. He restoreth my soul: he leadeth me in the paths of righteousness for his name's sake."* Take the full responsibility of how you hear the voice of God (your inception level), how you react after hearing His voice (your reception level) & how you accommodate the Word of God as it comes to you (your maturity level) for these three are keys that will unlock how far you are going to progress in this life! *Master these three responsibilities i.e. inception (knowledge and discretion), reception (understanding) and maturity (wisdom).* Proverbs 2:6 says & I quote, *"For the Lord giveth wisdom: out of his mouth cometh knowledge and understanding."*

APRIL EDITION

Theme: Clean Hands
(Job 17:19)

3rd Day

"Nevertheless, the righteous will hold to his way, & he who has clean hands will grow stronger and stronger."

> ## PROGRESS CONFESSION:
> *The blessing of the Lord is upon my life! I'm blessed & highly favored! My hands are clean in & out of season! Fruitfulness & multiplication are my daily*

Let this be your motive today to have clean hands for those that have clean hands are going to grow stronger & stronger. What are the clean hands being talking about here? Clean hands are the hands of people that are going to start business, career, ministry & or a project without any blood shed be it blood of an animal or that of a human being. You have to make up your mind that no matter what happens in this life I'm never going to use any charm nor do any ritual for me to start something. Desire to start small even though dreaming big! The Word of God says the Lord will bless the works of your hands (not just hands but clean hands)! Deuteronomy 28:8 says & I quote, *"The Lord shall command the blessing upon thee in thy storehouses & in all that thou settest thine hand unto & he shall bless thee in the land which the Lord thy God giveth thee."* Deuteronomy 7:13 says & I quote, *"And He'll love thee & bless thee & multiply thee: He'll also bless the fruit of thy womb & the fruit of thy land, thy corn & thy wine & thine oil, the increase of thy kine & the flocks of thy sheep, in the land which he sware unto thy fathers to give thee."* The degree of the cleanliness of your hands determines the level of the blessing you are to get from the Lord. Blessings come in levels (& or dimensions)! Some blessings are in levels (& or dimensions) in which even the devil himself dares not to tamper with them. Proverbs 10:22 says & I quote, *"The blessing of the Lord, it maketh rich & He addeth no sorrow with it."* The blessing of God that adds no sorrow with it is coming upon you now! You are going to be much stronger than before! You are an eagle & you are not going to get tired nor get weary but you are going to mount up your wings & soar higher (Isaiah 40:30-31). I prophesy a spirit of excellence to follow you starting today onwards! May you start to soar to higher levels in your academics, social life, finances, ministry, health, calling etc! The grace to make money & impact is therefore released to you! Watch out for the unleashing of new transitions now!

APRIL EDITION

Theme: Growing
Up In All Aspects
(Ephesians 4:15)

4th Day

"But speaking the truth in love, we are to grow up in all aspects into Him who is the head, even Christ."

> ## PROGRESS CONFESSION:
> *I'm going to know & speak the truth only for it is the truth that will definitely make me free! All I need to have in this life they can be unlocked through my*

For your progress to manifest in a rapid way, you have to learn to speak the truth in a lovely manner. And this truth will make you free! How will you be made free! By just speaking out that truth! John 8:32 says & I quote, *"And ye shall know the truth & the truth shall make you free."* Never provoke anyone through your speaking! Let your speech be gracious! Colossians 4:6 says & I quote, *"Let your speech be always with grace, seasoned with salt, that ye may know how ye ought to answer every man."* Let your speech be balanced (thus, showing growth in all aspects till you reach the Christ's level)! Know where & how to answer each & every person as they come! Allow your mouth (tongue) to be seasoned with salt! You are the salt & light of the earth! Matthewa 5:13-16 says & I quote, *"Ye are the salt of the earth: but if the salt has lost his savour, wherewith shall it be salted? it is thenceforth good for nothing, but to be cast out & to be trodden under foot of men. Ye are the light of the world. A city that is set on a hill cannot be hid. Neither do men light a candle & put it under a bushel, but on a candlestick & it giveth light unto all that are in the house. Let your light so shine before men, that they may see your good works & glorify your Father which is in heaven."* Season the earth through saying the truth & doing the correct things always! Death & life of your business, ministry, calling, health, career etc. all lies in the power of your tongue! Proverbs 18:21 says & I quote, *"Death & life are in the power of the tongue & they that love it shall eat the fruit thereof."* Allow the Holy Spirit to give you utterance! Acts 2:4 says & I quote, *"And they were all filled with the Holy Ghost & began to speak with other tongues, as the Spirit gave them utterance."* Don't just speak! Study the people & environment around you before you start to speak anything be it your social life, business, career, calling & or ministry! Luke 21:15 says & I quote, *"For I'll give you a mouth & wisdom, which all your adversaries shall not be able to gainsay nor resist."* No more contradictions! No more resistance! I prophesy that great deals are coming your way now! Be seasoned & strategic in your speech! Be professional! Dress the way you want to be addressed! Speak the way you want to be addressed as! Don't just dress or speak anyhow! You're big!

APRIL EDITION

Theme: From Glory
To Glory

(2 Corinthians 3:18)

5th Day

*"But we all, with unveiled face, beholding as in a mirror
the glory of the Lord, are being transformed into the same image from glory to glory,
just as from the Lord, the Spirit."*

> ## PROGRESS CONFESSION:
> *My life is moving from glory to glory! Everything
> around & about me are all going up! Nothing is going
> down & shall never go down! Upward & forward ever!*

Let this revelation & understanding sink in you that your life in Christ has to be from glory to glory. This is only found in Christ where the just live by faith (Galatians 3:11). Romans 1:17 says & I quote, *"For therein is the righteousness of God revealed from faith to faith: as it is written, the just shall live by faith."* The just are those people that are in Christ & are able to see Him face to face (for they are clean & free from sin because their sins are already forgiven) for there are no longer slaves but brothers & sisters to Christ (through adoption). Through adoption we behold as in a mirror the glory of God as we will be being transformed into the same image from glory to glory. Whatever you are doing, be it social life, business life, ministry life etc. adopt yourself into it (create a space in your business for you to understand it better so as to lead & control well). Create in you a space for your business till it you & that business you (become one) aren't separable to each other (thus being transformed into the same image). This will help you to run your business well & keep shining. Proverbs 4:18 says & I quote, *"But the path of the just is as the shining light, that shineth more & more unto the perfect day."* You shall never go down for your path is going to be like a dawn shining light that has to continue shining unto (until) the perfect day. Your business is rising up! This is the right time for great exploits! Your calling is uniquely taking shape & diversifying! This is your season & month to have a rapid progress! Your ministry is expanding! I prophesy that new permanent members & new branches are coming your way! Your marriage (relationship) is going forward! All about you are going to move from glory to glory! God bless you!

APRIL EDITION

Theme: Be Confident

(Philippians 1:6)

6th Day

"Being confident of this, that he who began a good work in you will carry it on to completion until the day of Christ Jesus."

PROGRESS CONFESSION:

I'm blessed with an eternal blessing of the Lord! I'm confident in the Lord who blessed me for He has good plans over my life besides me having His blessing!

Fear not! Just be glad & rejoice in the Lord for the Lord is doing marvellous things for you (Joel 2:21). Joel 2:23-24 says & I quote, *"Be glad then, ye children of Zion & rejoice in the Lord your God: for he hath given you the former rain moderately & he'll cause to come down for you the rain, the former rain & the latter rain in the first month. And the floors shall be full of wheat & the vats shall overflow with wine & oil."* Worry not about anything for everything is under control! Your floors & vats are going to be full of all the provisions you might ever need or want! Everything you might ever need or want; all has been put on a plan & has already been provided for by God! Joel 2:19 says & I quote, *"Yea, the Lord will answer & say unto his people, behold, I'll send you corn & wine & oil & ye shall be satisfied there-with: & I'll no more make you a reproach among the heathen."* He already has not just a plan, but rather plans for us! Jeremiah 29:11 says & I quote, *"For I know the thoughts that I think toward you, saith the Lord, thoughts of peace, and not of evil, to give you an expected end."* A better future & a hope (an expected end) is your portion! None of your visons (missions & destinies) shall be aborted nor miscarry by any means! Whatever you started, whichever way you go, the end report is that it is going to end well in a praise mode! You are not going to struggle for the grace & blessings have already been released upon your life! The Lord has already given you power to get wealth! It's now up to you to go out there & make use of the already available resources in a bid to make your wealth tangible. We are in Canaan & like the former Israel, the day we crossed River Jordan into Canaan, supernatural provision of quelea birds & manna ceased for we become the miracle ourselves! Wherever we are to go, we are to distribute miracles there! I prophesy in the name of Jesus Christ, let there be a miracle in your business, social life, ministry, calling, marriage & or relationship in the name of Jesus Christ! Money is coming! Money you haven't touched for years is about to fall into your hands! Be expectant & ready to enter a new level of finances for you carry the blessing of God! Proverbs 10:22 says & I quote, *"The blessing of the Lord, it maketh rich, and He addeth no sorrow with it."*

APRIL EDITION

Theme: Be Proactive
(1 Peter 2:1-3)

7th Day

"Therefore, rid yourselves of all malice & all deceit, hypocrisy, envy & slander of every kind. Like new born babies, crave pure spiritual milk, so that by it you may grow up in your salvation, now that you have tasted that the Lord is good."

> ## PROGRESS CONFESSION:
> *Through my daily meditation of the Word of God, my reactiveness is much more enhanced! Through the Word, I become more proactive, prosperous &*

As you will be growing big in your social life circles, business circles, ministry circles & so forth get rid of all malice, deceit, hypocrisy, envy & slander. Start to be busy for any small & fruitless talks. Start to tell yourself that you are no longer interested in time consuming yet fruitless talks. Tell yourself that you will never ever settle for less! Crave for the milk & cream as far as your trade (specialty) is concerned! Go for the best! Do your best & let God do the rest! When God created you, He created you in His image & after His own likeness for you to do the best like Him. He created you with a mandate for you to excel in everything you are to do or touch! He gave you a chance to taste Him & see how good He is. Psalm 34:8 says & I quote, *"O taste & see that the Lord is good: blessed is the man that trusteth in him."* Stay in the Word of God & let the Word give you direction! Eat His Word for it sweeter than honey! Psalm 119:103-105 says & I quote, *"How sweet are thy words unto my taste! Yea, sweeter than honey to my mouth! Through thy precepts I get understanding: therefore, I hate every false way. Thy word is a lamp unto my feet, & a light unto my path."* The Word has the capacity to bring light into your life, business, marriage & or ministry! Psalm 119:130 says & I quote, *"The entrance of thy words giveth light; it giveth understanding unto the simple."* The Word of God will give you light *(thus, best knowledge, unmatched wisdom & greater understanding)* fit for you to do great exploits. Meditate upon the Word of God; day in, day out; night in, night out – this will make your way prosperous & you will have good success. Meditation will help you to be more proactive as far as your social life (business, ministry, calling & or marriage) principles are concerned! Joshua 1:7-8 says & I quote, *"Only be thou strong and very courageous, that thou mayest observe to do according to all the law, which Moses my servant commanded thee: turn not from it to the right hand or to the left, that thou mayest prosper withersoever thou goest. This book of the law shall not depart out of thy mouth; but thou shalt meditate therein day & night, that thou may observe to do according to all that is written therein: for then thou shalt make thy way prosperous, and then thou shalt have good success."*

8th Day

"So that you may live a life worthy of the Lord and please him in every way: bearing fruit in every good work, growing in the knowledge of God."

PROGRESS CONFESSION:

I have made up my mind that I'm going to be willing & obedient to the Word of God! I'm going to diligently seek God's face & do whatever His Word dictates!

The goal is to first live a life worthy of the Lord till God is pleased with our lives so that He may reward us with each & every kind of the blessing the Lord has in store for us. 1 Corinthians 2:9 says & I quote, *"But as it is written, Eye hath not seen, nor ear heard, neither have entered into the heart of man, the things which God hath prepared for them that love him."* Diligently seek after the Lord's face & His Word! Hebrews 11:6 says & I quote, *"But without faith it is impossible to please him: for he that cometh to God must believe that he is, & that he is a rewarder of them that diligently seek him."* Have faith in the Lord, be obedient to His Word & be willing to receive His blessings! Isaiah 1:19 says & I quote, *"If ye be willing and obedient, ye shall eat the good of the land."* For you to bear good fruit, you have to be willing first! It is out of your willingness that your fruitfulness is bound to emanate from. Good apples always come from a willing apple tree – the one that is not willing will never give you good apples. Likewise good results always come out of a willing man's life. Be willing to break records this year & by default you shall surely do so. Odds are only defied by willing minds. *Willingness equals fruitfulness!* Whatsoever you want to see happening in your life (be it socially, financially, spiritually & physically), be willing to see it happening. Our Lord, Jesus Christ, he became willing first way before He even cleansed that leper on Mark 1:40-41 which says & I quote, *"And there came a leper to him, beseeching him, & kneeling down to him, & saying unto him, if thou wilt, thou canst make me clean. And Jesus, moved with compassion, put forth his hand, & touched him, & saith unto him, I'll; be thou clean."* Your willing-ness has a reward and it brings life to each and everything that concerns you. 1 Corinthians 9:17 says & I quote, *"For if I do this thing willingly, I have a reward: but if against my will, a dispensation of the gospel is committed unto me."* 2 Corinthians 8:12 says & I quote, *"For if there be first a willing mind, it is accepted according to that a man has, not according to that he hasn't."*

APRIL EDITION

Theme: Growing Roots
(Colossians 2:7)

9th Day

"Let your roots grow down into Him, & let your lives be built on Him. Then your faith will grow strong in the truth you were taught, & you will overflow with thankfulness."

> ## PROGRESS CONFESSION:
> *I'm growing deeper roots into my business through faith in my Lord Jesus Christ! From glory to glory I'm moving & I'm not going to stop! I'm forever shining!*

There is an overflow coming into your life! Business ideas are going to flood in your mind! Money is going to flood your money bags, wallets, pockets & your bank accounts! You shall never lack money for in the day you will have little cash in your hands, the gifts God bestowed you with are going to cause money to be attracted to you! You shall effortlessly make millions! *Money that is coming now is no longer for hand to mouth purposes but it's money for you to settle down (thus, being stable & solid)! Money that is coming now is for you to grow roots! Money that is coming now is for you to invest in real estate business!* You shall have tangible assets! You shall buy houses & cars like tomatoes & onions! You shall buy new properties like relish! Nothing shall be too expensive for you to buy for you are going to have excess money! Many nations (people) shall feed from your hands! You shall never lack for you shall be grounded in the Lord! As you will be helping others, God is going to help you as well. As you will be praying for your friends, the Lord is going to restore all your losses! Job 42:10 says & I quote, *"And the Lord turned the captivity of Job, when he prayed for his friends: also, the Lord gave Job twice as much as he had before."* Joel 2:24-26 says & I quote, *"And the floors shall be full of wheat, & the vats shall overflow with wine & oil. And I'll restore to you the years that the locust hath eaten, the cankerworm, & the caterpillar, & the palmerworm, my great army which I sent among you. And ye shall eat in plenty, & be satisfied, and praise the name of the Lord your God, that hath dealt wondrously with you: & my people shall never be ashamed."* Your faith is going to be strong & you're going to move mountains. Any mountain that is to refuse to be moved by the words of your mouth, it's going to melt down. I prophesy the loss of power to any sickness, stagnation, bankruptcy, conspiracy, & hindrance that may come against your progress! You are going to move from glory to glory! You are going to shine like never before! Proverbs 4:18 says & I quote, *"But the path of the just is as the shining light, that shineth more and more unto the perfect day."* 2 Corinthians 3:18 says & I quote, *"But we all, with open face beholding as in a glass the glory of the Lord, are changed into the same image from glory to glory, even as by the Spirit of the Lord."*

APRIL EDITION

Theme: Enlarging Tents
(Isaiah 54:2-3)

10th Day

"Enlarge the place of your tent, stretch your tent curtains wide, do not hold back; lengthen your cords, strengthen your stakes. For you will spread out to the right and to the left; your descendants will dispossess nations and settle in their desolate cities."

> ## PROGRESS CONFESSION:
> *My financial capacity is increasing on a daily basis! My economical value is ever increasing from glory to glory! I'm now living luxuriously like a king (& a*

Wow! This is the right time for you to expand your business, properties & even your spiritual life (ministry or calling). Enlarge the place of your tents, but remember not to do alone (rather do so with the aid of our Lord Jesus Christ). Allow Him to be on the lead! Let Him be the one to stretch your tent curtains wide & don't hold back but lengthen your cords & then strengthen your stakes. Genesis 13:14-18 says & I quote, *"And the Lord said unto Abram, after that Lot was separated from him, lift up now thine eyes, & look from the place where thou art northward, & southward, & eastward, & westward: for all the land which thou seest, to thee will I give it, & to thy seed for ever. And I'll make thy seed as the dust of the earth: so that if a man can number the dust of the earth, then shall thy seed also be numbered. Arise, walk through the land in the length of it & in the breadth of it; for I'll give it unto thee. Then Abram removed his tent, and came and dwelt in the plain of Mamre, which is in Hebron, & built there an altar unto the Lord."* As far as you can see (imagine, think, envision & or desire) is that which the Lord has given unto you! Proverbs 23:7 says & I quote, *"As a man thinketh in his heart, so is he."* What are you think of today? Whatever & whichever thing you are thinking of, God is going to make that thing a reality to you & in your life or else you are to become that thing or person you're thinking of becoming! Enlargement is coming! In the journey or process to your enlargement season, if you are to face rejection or any hindrance (obstacle), don't get carried away or get discouraged but rather be positive for each & every rejection is always escorted by a redirection to your destiny! 2 Kings 6:1-7 says & I quote, *"And the sons of the prophets said unto Elisha, behold, now the place where we dwell with thee is too strait for us. Let us go, we pray thee, unto Jordan, & take thence every man a beam, & let us make us a place there, where we may dwell. And he answered, Go ye. And one said, be content, I pray thee, & go with thy servants. And he answered, I will go. So, he went with them. And when they came to Jordan, they cut down wood. But as one was felling a beam, the axe head fell into the water: & he cried, & said, alas, master! for it was borrowed. And the man of God said, where fell it? And he shewed him the place. And he cut down a stick, & cast it in thither; & the iron did swim. Therefore, said he, take it up to thee. And he put out his hand, & took it."* Enlargement comes with resistance & rejection but we have our Master Strategist – Jesus Christ who overcame resistance & rejection effortlessly. I prophesy in the name of Jesus Christ that wherever you face resistance before, smooth passage has been activated! Wherever you faced rejection before, VIP acceptance. Favor is being released now! Received favor & grace to manoeuvre in the market places! Your applications are all going to be accepted! Your bids are going to be successful! Grace to make money has been activated into your life & spirit now!

APRIL EDITION

Theme: Press On
(Philippians 3:13-14)

11th Day

"Brothers & sisters, I do not consider myself yet to have taken hold of it. But one thing I do: Forgetting what is behind & straining toward what is ahead, I press on toward the goal to win the prize for which God has called me heavenward in Christ Jesus."

> ## PROGRESS CONFESSION:
> *I'm pressing on towards the goal of having the first prize! I'm destined to the number 1 & not number 2 or 3! The first spot is mine! I'm by default "His*

If you really want to progress in life, you have to learn not to consider yourself a winner before the race. Yes, being confident of yourself is good but being humble its far much better, worse off trusting in the Lord is the best. Psalm 37:4-6 says & I quote, *"Delight thyself also in the Lord: & he shall give thee the desires of thine heart. Commit thy way unto the Lord; trust also in him; and he shall bring it to pass. And he shall bring forth thy righteousness as the light, & thy judgment as the noonday."* Proverbs 3:5 says & I quote, *"Trust in the Lord with all thine heart; & lean not unto thine own understanding."* Trusting in the Lord means forgetting that which is behind & straining towards that which is in the future. Press on towards having a better life! Press on towards having a better end (Jeremiah 29:11)! Press on towards building a long-lasting legacy! Press on towards having generational wealth! Proverbs 13:22 says & I quote, *"A good man leaveth an inheritance to his children's children: and the wealth of the sinner is laid up for the just."* Go after excellence! Pursue excellence till it becomes part of your normal routine! Let people know you as the par excellence guy in everything you do! Whatever you're to find yourself doing, do it with mightiness (Ecclesiastes 9:10)! If you're to sing, sing with excellence & mightiness! If you're to pray, pray with excellence & mightiness! If you're to do your job, work with excellence & mightiness! If you're to start a business, do so with excellence & mightiness! I pray for you, it's done!

APRIL EDITION

Theme: Love Abound

(Philippians 1:9-11)

12th Day

"And this is my prayer: that your love may abound more &
more in knowledge & depth of insight, so that you may be able to discern what is best
and may be pure and blameless for the day of Christ, filled with the fruit of
righteousness that comes through
Jesus Christ – to the glory and praise of God."

> ## PROGRESS CONFESSION:
> *I'm forever pursuing love for in the abundance of love thus where unity & progress are found! Purity is my daily portion! I'm pure & blameless in Christ Jesus'*

Wow!

What a great prayer our Apostle Paul did for us & the generations that are to come! He prayed that you & me, our love for each other has to abound & as it abounds, our knowledge & the depth of our insight has to increase as well such that we may be able to discern that which is best for us, to us & with us. Pursue purity & be blameless for out of it lies many spiritual & physical blessings. Isaiah 1:19 says & I quote, *"If ye be willing and obedient, ye shall eat the good of the land."* Be filled with the fruit of righteousness that comes through Christ. Proverbs 10:22 says & I quote, *"The blessing of the Lord, it maketh rich, and he addeth no sorrow with it."* What attracts this blessing of the Lord? It is your ability to obedient & willing to God's voice (& or word). In other words, thus having faith in God. Hebrews 11:1-6 says & I quote, *"Now faith is the substance of things hoped for, the evidence of things not seen. For by it the elders obtained a good report. Through faith we understand that the worlds were framed by the word of God, so that things which are seen were not made of things which do appear. By faith Abel offered unto God a more excellent sacrifice than Cain, by which he obtained witness that he was righteous, God testifying of his gifts: and by it he being dead yet speaketh. By faith Enoch was translated that he should not see death; & was not found, because God had translated him: for before his translation he had this testimony, that he pleased God. But without faith it is impossible to please him: for he that cometh to God must believe that he is, and that he is a rewarder of them that diligently seek him."* Once the Lord's blessing has rested upon you & your life, you have to let love lead. Help those around you to be like you or even to be more than you.

Real eagles allow their poor eaglets to fly above them so that the poor eaglets can start to develop strong minds that they can even do better than their senior eagles. Start to see beyond the current situation at hand! Start to see that poor guy you are seeing today as the future CEO of a big corporate tomorrow! See the unseen with love abound eyes! Love covers a multitude of sins, so you have to embrace it so as to win all & in everything in this life.

APRIL EDITION

**Theme: Bearing
Much Fruit**
(John 15:5)

13th Day

"I am the vine; you are the branches. If you remain in me & I in you, you will bear much fruit; apart from me you can do nothing."

PROGRESS CONFESSION:
This year & starting this month, I'm going to be bearing much fruit! Much fruit at home! Much fruit at work! Much fruit at church! Much fruit in business! For you to bear much fruit in this life (physical world), you have to be in Christ. What is being in Christ? This is done in you having to put all your trust in Christ, thus a 100% dependency on Him in everything. Jeremiah 29:11 says & I quote, *"For I know the thoughts that I think toward you, saith the Lord, thoughts of peace, & not of evil, to give you an expected end."* Philippians 4:13 says & I quote, *"I can do all things through Christ which strengthens me."* Put all your trust & have faith in God for He is the one that gives people power to get wealth (Deuteronomy 8:18). Wealth is not made but rather it has to be gotten. What is made is you being rich by the blessing of God (Proverbs 10:22). For wealth to come to you, you have to have certain power (& authority) for huge wealth gravitates towards certain powers (authorities, levels, names & or positions). And as of you, kindly note this that you're already seated with Christ in heavenly places far above principalities, powers & rulers of this world (Ephesians 1:19-23). Ephesians 1:22 says & I quote, *"And hath put all things under his feet, & gave him to be the head over all things to the church."* All is under your feet! You're the head & never a tail! You're set high above many nations! You're blessed in & out of city! Much fruit is your portion! Deuteronomy 28:3-6 says & I quote, *"Blessed shalt thou be in the city, & blessed shalt thou be in the field. Blessed shall be the fruit of thy body, and the fruit of thy ground, & the fruit of thy cattle, the increase of thy kine, & the flocks of thy sheep. Blessed shall be thy basket & thy store. Blessed shalt thou be when thou comest in, & blessed shalt thou be when thou goest out."* Isaiah 60:5-6 says & I quote, *"Then thou shalt see, and flow together & thine heart shall fear & be enlarged; because the abundance of the sea shall be converted unto thee, the forces of the Gentiles shall come*

unto thee...multitude of camels shall cover thee, the dromedaries of Midian & Ephah; all they from Sheba shall come: they shall bring gold & incense; & they shall shew forth the praises of the Lord."

APRIL EDITION

Theme: Character & Hope

(Romans 5:3-5)

14th Day

*"Not only so, but we also glory in our sufferings, because we
know that suffering produces perseverance; perseverance, character
and character, hope. And hope does not put us to shame, because God's love has been
poured out into our hearts through the
Holy Spirit, who has been given to us."*

PROGRESS CONFESSION:

*I'm going to be working on my character & hope on a
daily basis! Out of my character, I will get much
wealth, will make many riches & build up many*

Permanent progress in life is directly proportional to your personal character & hope you have about your life (& the coming future). Troubles, hindrances, obstacles, mishaps temptations, sufferings & fights are going to come but try by all means to be positive for it is your positivity in suffering that paves your way out of it. Positivity in a hot battle give you victory always! Positivity moulds your character & gives hope, no matter the situation. King Jehoshaphat when the battle became tense, he was told by Prophet Jahaziel that the battle wasn't his but the Lord's. He believed it & it happened! He positively welcomed the Prophet's words & hope for victory was activated. 2 Chronicles 20:15-17 says & I quote, *"And he said, Hearken, ye all Judah, & ye inhabitants of Jerusalem, & thou king Jehoshaphat, thus saith the Lord unto you, be not afraid nor dismayed by reason of this great multitude; for the battle is not yours, but God's. Tomorrow go ye down against them: behold, they come up by the cliff of Ziz; & ye shall find them at the end of the brook, before the wilderness of Jeruel. Ye shall not need to fight in this battle: set yourselves, stand ye still, & see the salvation of the Lord with you, O Judah & Jerusalem: fear not, nor be dismayed; tomorrow go out against them: for the Lord will be with you."* Be humble & allow God to do what He know to suite you the best way. Safeguard your heart (character) diligent for out of it flows issues of life. Proverbs 4:23 says & I quote, *"Keep thy heart with all diligence; for out of it are the issues of life."* A good name is better than precious ointment (Ecclesiastes 7:1). Proverbs 22:1 says & I quote, *"A good name is rather to be chosen than great riches, & loving favour rather than silver & gold."* Do all these whilst safeguarding your spirit & hope. Proverbs 17:22 says & I quote, *"A merry heart doeth good like a medicine: but a broken spirit drieth the bones."* Proverbs 18:14 says & I quote, *"The spirit of a man will sustain his infirmity; but a wounded spirit who can bear?"* Proverbs 13:12 says & I quote, *"Hope deferred maketh the heart sick: but when the desire cometh, it is a tree of life."*

APRIL EDITION

**Theme: The Aliveness
of The Word of God**
(Hebrews 4:12)

15th Day

"For the word of God is alive and active. Sharper than any double-edged sword, it penetrates even to dividing soul & spirit, joints & marrow; it judges the thoughts and attitudes of the heart."

PROGRESS CONFESSION:

Nothing is sharper than the Word of God here on earth! The Word of God is alive in me & I'm in the Word of God as well! I live & move by the Word of

The amount of the Word of God alive & active in you, determines your level of greatness & impact you are going to make in this life. Speak out the Word of God! Proverbs 6:2 says & I quote, *"Thou art snared with the words of thy mouth, thou art taken with the words of thy mouth."* If by the words of your mouth, you can get snared, I believe also that by the words of your mouth, you can get your freedom. The words of your mouth can make you to be taken (accepted, married, employed, befriended, loved, helped etc.) for they will have been seasoned by the Word of God. Learn to speak graciously to anyone; whether big or small, dirty or smart, rich or poor etc. Just be gracious & generous to all for you never know what tomorrow is carrying for you. A beggar on the street today might be your employer tomorrow! Learn to discern spirits from souls & marrow from joints! Make use of the Word of God in you to transform you, your life & the world around you! Psalm 107:20 says & I quote, *"He sent his word & healed then & delivered them from their destructions."* Allow the Word of God help you to heal from your toxic past experiences (negative situations & events) that have made you to be bitter & hurt. Allow the Word of God to judge & clean all of your thoughts & attitudes towards life & your future way before you start executing them. Healing is coming! And progress is also coming for it is healing that gives birth to permanent progress. God bless you, shalom.

APRIL EDITION

Theme: Mind Renewal
(Romans 12:2)

16th Day

"Do not conform to the pattern of this world, but be transformed by the renewing of your mind. Then you will be able to test & approve what God's will is – his good, pleasing and perfect will.

PROGRESS CONFESSION:
My mind has been renewed! I'm now thinking differently & with new goals! My plans are now in synchrony with God's plans for He is in me & He is

At times for you to progress well in this life, you have to have a renewed mind – a mindset that is not limited by the systems of this world. You have to be someone that is not conformed to the pattern & systems of this world but live far above the patterns & systems of this world. You have to appreciate the fact that Christ is in you & He is in you not for the now moment only but forever! Colossians 1:26-27 says & I quote, *"Even the mystery which hath been hid from ages and from generations, but now is made manifest to his saints: to whom God would make known what is the riches of the glory of this mystery among the Gentiles; which is Christ in you, the hope of glory."* You have to also acknowledge the fact that the Spirit of God that raised Jesus from the dead is now in you. Nothing in you & around you is ever going to die! The resurrection power in you will revive everything back to life. God once us to live according to His will (thus, His plans for our lives). Jeremiah 29:11 which says & I quote, *"For I know the thoughts that I think toward you, saith the Lord, thoughts of peace, and not of evil, to give you an expected end."* In His plans, you will never fail! In His plans, you will never fall! In His plans, you will never stumble! In His plans, you will never struggle nor beg! Psalm 37:25 says & I quote, *"I have been young, and now am old; yet have I not seen the righteous forsaken, nor his seed begging bread."*

APRIL EDITION

Theme: Chosen From
The Beginning
(2 Thessalonians 2:13)

17th Day

"But we should always give thanks to God for you, brethren beloved by the Lord, because God has chosen you from the beginning for salvation through sanctification by the Spirit & faith in the truth."

> ## PROGRESS CONFESSION:
> *I'm a chosen one of God! I'm a peculiar & holy person full of all the capabilities & abilities of God in me! I'm a small god! I'm God & God is in me! Hallelujah!*

Wow! What a remarkable compliment & or attribute you have as a believer in Christ that the Lord has already chosen you & me to be part of His family. We're part of Him & Him part of us by election! There was an election that happened before the foundations of the earth were established. The electorate was given million options to chose from & yet they chose you. You're a chosen general of God! You're a peculiar breed, thus the God kind (Psalm 82:6). 1 Peter 2:9 says & I quote, *"But ye are a chosen generation, a royal priesthood, a holy nation, a peculiar people; that ye should shew forth the praises of him who hath called you out of darkness into his marvellous light."* God called you out of darkness into His marvellous light before we were formed in our mothers' wombs. Jeremiah 1:5 says & I quote, *"Before I formed thee in the belly I knew thee; and before thou camest forth out of the womb I sanctified thee, and I ordained thee a prophet unto the nations."* Be holy & perfect for your Master is holy & perfect. 1 Peter 1:13-16 says & I quote, *"Wherefore gird up the loins of your mind, be sober & hope to the end for the grace that is to be brought unto you at the revelation of Jesus Christ; as obedient children, not fashioning yourselves according to the former lusts in your ignorance: but as he which hath called you is holy, so be ye holy in all manner of conversation; because it is written, be ye holy; for I am holy."* We're the predestined sons of God (Ephesians 1:5) & we're awaiting our full manifestation in this world (Romans 8:19). God adopted us from the onset of the world, thus why He gave us the Spirit of Adoption & not of bondage (Romans 8:15). 2 Timothy 1:7 says & I quote, *"For God hath not given us the spirit of fear; but of power & of love & of a sound mind."* 1 Timothy 3:16 says & I quote, *"And without controversy great is the mystery of godliness: God was manifest in the flesh, justified in the Spirit, seen of angels, preached unto the Gentiles, believed on in the world, received up into glory."*

APRIL EDITION

Theme: Are You Ready?
(1 Corinthians 3:1-3)

18th Day

"Brothers & sisters, I could not address you as people who live by the Spirit but as people who are still worldly – mere infants in Christ. I gave you milk, not solid food, for you were not yet ready for it. Indeed, you are still not ready. You are still worldly. For since there is jealousy & quarrelling among you, are you not worldly?
Are you not acting like mere humans?"

> ## PROGRESS CONFESSION:
> I'm now ready to let go petty issues & move forward!
> I'm now ready to increase my capacity both in giving
> & in receiving! Superior expertise is my ultimate goal!

In whatever you are to do, you have to learn & graduate from being an infant into brothers & sister do that you start to work for your own salvation. Children (infants in Christ) are the ones that are supposed to be provided milk & not solid food by God. Grow up into a bigger person for better things to start happening to you! Grow into a bigger person for better benefits to start flocking down to you! Your capacity matters most to God! Before God starts dishing out His blessings to you, He first take a survey of your capacity. Are you able to contain His blessings for His blessing makes one rich & adds no sorrow with it? Proverbs 10:22 says & I quote, *"The blessing of the Lord, it maketh rich, and he addeth no sorrow with it."* Be spiritual for the world is now more spiritual & at a more advanced stage for you to be physical. Hebrews 11:3 says & I quote, *"Through faith we understand that the worlds were framed by the word of God, so that things which are seen were not made of things which do appear."* Be willing to learn till you are an expert (thus, a guru)! Strive to be a skilful employee, employer, businessman, businesswoman, minister, parent etc. Hebrews 5:12-14 says & I quote, *"For when for the time ye ought to be teachers, ye've need that one teaches you again which be the first principles of the oracles of God & are become such as have need of milk & not of strong meat. For every one that useth milk is unskilful in the word of righteousness: for he is a babe. But strong meat belongeth to them that are of full age, even those who by reason of use have their senses exercised to discern both good & evil."* Be ready to be of full age now! Take a step now, do something new! This is the ripe time for you to go up & never to go down again.

APRIL EDITION

Theme: Go For Maturity
(Ephesians 4:13-15)

19th Day

"Until we all attain to the unity of the faith & of the knowledge of the Son of God, to a mature man, to the measure of the stature which belongs to the fullness of Christ. As a result, we are no longer to be children, tossed here and there by waves and carried about by every wind of doctrine, by the TRICKERY of men, by craftiness in deceitful scheming; but speaking the truth in love, we're to grow up in all aspects into Him who is the head, even Christ."

> ### PROGRESS CONFESSION:
> My goal is to be mature in everything that I'm doing & I'm going to be doing; be it business wise, social life, spiritually etc. I'm firmly rooted in my faith & core values! No more room for the to & fro tossing!

The Word of God today is saying that you have to go for & after maturity. Don't go after your own interests, needs & desires but go for the unity of faith & of the knowledge of the Son of God for you to do exploits. Daniel 11:32 says & I quote, *"And such as do wickedly against the covenant shall he corrupt by flatteries: but the people that do know their God shall be strong, & do exploits."* Philippians 2:1-4 says & I quote, *"If there be therefore any consolation in Christ, if any comfort of love, if any fellowship of the Spirit, if any bowels and mercies, fulfil ye my joy, that ye be likeminded, having the same love, being of one accord, of one mind. Let nothing be done through strife or vainglory; but in lowliness of mind let each esteem other better than themselves. Look not every man on his own things, but every man also on the things of others."* Go for maturity & stay in that maturity for maturity is the ability to study, understand & respect personality differences. Learn to study, understand & master differences in ministries, trades, jobs, businesses etc. so as to respect the differences & to be taken away. Learn to speak the truth in love for you to be free & grow well. John 8:32 says & I quote, *"And ye shall know the truth, and the truth shall make you free."* Be mature in your understanding of the truth for it is in your maturity in the understanding of the truth that your rapid progress is permanently lying. 1 Corinthians 14:20 says & I quote,

"Brethren, be not children in understanding: howbeit in malice be ye children, but in understanding be men."

<u>APRIL EDITION</u>

Theme: Perseverance
(Luke 8:14-15)

20th Day

"The seed which fell among the thorns, these are the ones who have heard & as they go on their way they're choked with worries & riches & pleasures of this life & bring no fruit to maturity. But the seed in the good soil, these are the ones who have heard the word in an honest & good heart & hold it fast & bear fruit with perseverance."

> ## PROGRESS CONFESSION:
> *I'm persevering always & out of my perseverance; I'm going to bear much fruit! Forward ever, backward never! I'm holy! I'm rich! I'm blessed! I'm highly*

If you really desire to be great & go far in life, have an honest & good heart towards the Word of God holding to it fast so as to bear fruits with perseverance. Do whatever the Word says you have to do! Mary on the wedding at Canna told them they were to do whatever He (Jesus Christ) was to tell them. John 2:5 says & I quote, *"His mother saith unto the servants, 'Whatsoever he saith unto you, do it.'"* Joshua 1:5-8 says & I quote, *"There shall not any man be able to stand before thee all the days of thy life: as I was with Moses, so I'll be with thee: I'll not fail thee, nor forsake thee. Be strong & of a good courage: for unto this people shalt thou divide for an inheritance the land, which I sware unto their fathers to give them. Only be thou strong & very courageous, that thou mayest observe to do according to all the law, which Moses my servant commanded thee: turn not from it to the right hand or to the left, that thou mayest prosper withersoever thou goest. This book of the law shall not depart out of thy mouth; but thou shalt meditate therein day and night, that thou mayest observe to do according to all that is written therein: for then thou shalt make thy way prosperous, and then thou shalt have good success."* Refuse to stop for no man shall be able to stand before you all the days of your life! Refuse to stop for the Lord is not going to be with you always! Refuse to stop for the Lord has better plans for you (Jeremiah 29:11). Jeremiah 33:3 says & I quote, *"Call unto me, and I will answer thee, & show thee great & mighty things, which thou knowest not."* Be strong & courageous for out of your strength & courage God shall let you divide this land (material things) as your inheritance. Keep on going forward, never stop nor get weary! The Lord knows you & you know

Him as well! If you really know God, the great exploits are going to be your daily portion (Daniel 11:32). Isaiah 40:29-31 says & I quote, *"He giveth power to the faint; and to them that have no might he increaseth strength. Even the youths shall faint and be weary, and the young men shall utterly fall: but they that wait upon the Lord shall renew their strength; they shall mount up with wings as eagles; they shall run, and not be weary; and they shall walk, and not faint."*

APRIL EDITION

Theme: Mustard Seed
(Matthew 13:31-32)

21st Day

"The kingdom of heaven is like a mustard seed, which a man took & planted in his field. Though it is the smallest of all seeds, yet when it grows, it is the largest of garden plants and becomes a tree."

> ## PROGRESS CONFESSION:
> *This month, I'm going to move mountains! Chains & walls are falling right now! Gates & doors are opening right now! Chances are being created right now!*

Luke 6:38 says & I quote, *"Give, and it shall be given unto you; good measure, pressed down, and shaken together, and running over, shall men give into your bosom. For with the same measure that ye mete withal it shall be measured to you again."* Let this revelation sink in you that each & every giving is a seed. The size of the seed doesn't matter but that which germinates matters more than the seed itself for in it lies the life of many trees, fruits & seeds. Pastor Chris once said, 'One tree, a forest.' I came to prophesy that each & every gift you have given be it socially, mentally, emotionally, physically, economically, spiritually & or financially is going to yield into a fruitful tree! Learn to give for it is in your giving that certain doors that have been resistive are going to open. Genesis 22:9-18 says & I quote, *"And they came to the place which God had told him of & Abraham built an altar there & laid the wood in order and bound Isaac his son, and laid him on the altar upon the wood. And Abraham stretched forth his hand & took the knife to slay his son. And the angel of the Lord called unto him out of heaven & said, Abraham, Abraham & he said, here am I. And he said, lay not thine hand upon the lad, neither do thou anything unto him: for now, I know that thou fear God, seeing thou hast not withheld thy son, thine only son from me. And Abraham lifted up his eyes & looked & behold behind him a ram caught in a thicket by his horns & Abraham went & took the ram, and offered him up for a burnt offering in the stead of his son. And Abraham called the name of that place Jehovah Jireh: as it is said to this day, in the mount of the Lord it shall be seen. And the angel of the Lord called unto Abraham out of heaven the second time & said, by myself have I sworn, saith the Lord, for because thou hast done this thing & hast not withheld thy son, thine only son: that in blessing I'll bless thee*

& in multiplying I'll multiply thy seed as the stars of the heaven and as the sand which is upon the sea shore & thy seed shall possess the gate of his enemies & in thy seed shall all the nations of the earth be blessed; because thou hast obeyed my voice." Abraham sowed his seed unto the Lord & the returns were far much beyond his imaginations. He mastered this mystery that obeying God's voice is better than any sacrifice (1 Samuel 15:22). So, you have to go after obedience more than you pursue sacrifices! Proverbs 21:3 says & I quote, *"To do justice & judgment is more acceptable to the Lord than sacrifice."*

APRIL EDITION

Theme: Test Yourself
(2 Corinthians 13:5-7)

22nd Day

"Examine yourselves, to see whether you are in the faith. Test yourselves. Or do you not realize this about yourselves, that Jesus Christ is in you? – unless indeed you fail to meet the test! I hope you will find out that we have not failed the test. But we pray to God that you may not do wrong – not that we may appear to have met
the test, but that you may do what is right, though we may seem to have failed."

> ## PROGRESS CONFESSION:
> *I've fully examined myself, I'm in faith, with faith & of faith! Christ is in me & He is the hope of glory, power, life, healing, grace, riches, authority & excellence!*

For gold to be gold it has to be tested first & if the quality has not yet reached the required premium, it is returned back to the furnace. In other words, it's put in a closed oven (furnace) till it reaches a purity (excellence & or perfection) stage. Quality products are tested before they are put on the market, so the same analogy applies to us, we have to test ourselves before we make ourselves & our services before we start to make ourselves available to the market. Check your quality versus the quality of Christ is in you. Christ in you is not carnal, neither is He poor nor broke. He is rich & makes people become rich! Proverbs 10:22 says & I quote, *"The blessing of the Lord, it maketh rich & He addeth no sorrow with it."* He is wealth & gives people strength to get wealth! Deuteronomy 8:18 says & I quote, *"But thou shalt remember the Lord thy God: for it is He that giveth thee power to get wealth, that He may establish His covenant which he sware unto thy fathers, as it is this day."* The opening scripture says that you've not failed the test – meaning to say that you have already passed the test! Though it seems like the devil has won, your competitors are gaining much ground against you, you are having little income etc. the scripture is saying that you haven't faith for the Lord is with thee. Trials & tests may come but victory comes from the Lord & not the battlefield! I prophesy in the name of Jesus Christ that your success is imminent! You are not going to fail in all the tests & examinations you are to face in this life & that to come! Excellence is your portion! Perfection is your portion!

Theme: Abound In
Thanksgiving
(Colossians 2:6-7)

23rd Day

"Therefore, as you received Christ Jesus the Lord, so walk in him, rooted and built up in him & established in the faith, just as you were taught, abounding in thanksgiving."

PROGRESS CONFESSION:
I'm abounding in thanksgiving for I have mastered that it is abundance of thanksgiving that gives birth to my rising and greatness enhancement! I'm rising

After receiving Jesus Christ as your personal Savior, you have to note that Christianity is not a religion that is to be revered to one day of the week but rather it is a lifestyle that needs to be embraced & lived on a daily basis. Philippians 2:12 says & I quote, *"Wherefore, my beloved, as ye have always obeyed, not as in my presence only, but now much more in my absence, work out your own salvation with fear and trembling."* How do you work out your own salvation? This is done through you abounding in thanksgiving! Thanksgiving is not real if it's not coming from a platform of love. You have to love your neighbour the way you love your own self (Matthew 22:39 & Mark 12:31) for God is love (1 John 4:8). 1 John 4:16 says & I quote, *"And we have known and believed the love that God hath to us. God is love & he that dwelleth in love dwelleth in God & God in him."* If you want God to be with you always & you to be in God always, then let love lead! Faith is good, hope is good, sacrifice is good but love is the best! Love is the greatest of them all! In other words, love is a G.O.A.T – thus, the Greatest Of All Times! Romans 13:9 says & I quote, *"For this, thou shalt not commit adultery, thou shalt not kill, thou shalt not steal, thou shalt not bear false witness, thou shalt not covet & if there be any other commandment, it is briefly comprehended in this saying, namely, thou shalt love thy neighbour as thyself."* Jeremiah 30:19 says & I quote, *"And out of them shall proceed thanksgiving & the voice of them that make merry & I will multiply them and they shall not be few; I will also glorify them and they shall not be small."* Your permanent multiplication is fast approaching you! Your increment is coming for the Lord is glorifying you! You shall never be small but expansion is your daily portion! Your business is expanding now! Your life is being lengthened now! Your abilities are being multiplied now! From glory to glory you are moving now (Proverbs 4:18). God bless you.

APRIL EDITION

Theme: Ask The Lord
(Luke 17:5)

24th Day

"The apostles said to the Lord, "Increase our faith!""

> ## PROGRESS CONFESSION:
> *I'm increasing in my faith daily! I'm moving from glory to glory, power to power, grace to grace, dominion to dominion! Increase is my daily portion!*

Increase in your faith is coming but it has to be asked for. Go before the Lord today & ask for the increase of your faith. Faith comes by hearing & hearing by the Word of God (Romans 10:17). Habakkuk 2:4 says & I quote, *"Behold, his soul which is lifted up is not upright in him: but the just shall live by his faith."* Your life has to be centred on faith for we walk not by our own eyes (sight) but by our own faith (2 Corinthians 5:7). Faith heals! Matthew 9:22 says & I quote, *"But Jesus turned him about, and when he saw her, he said, daughter, be of good comfort; thy faith hath made thee whole. And the woman was made whole from that hour."* Matthew 15:28 says & I quote, *"Then Jesus answered & said unto her, O woman, great is thy faith: be it unto thee even as thou wilt. And her daughter was made whole from that very hour."* Faith open closed eyes (both physically & spiritually)! Matthew 9:29 says & I quote, *"Then touched he their eyes, saying, according to your faith be it unto you."* Faith moves mountains (situations) & make nothing impossible! Matthew 17:20 says & I quote, *"And Jesus said unto them, because of your unbelief: for verily I say unto you, if ye have faith as a grain of mustard seed, ye shall say unto this mountain, remove hence to yonder place & it shall remove; and nothing shall be impossible unto you."* Faith leads one to salvation! Luke 5:20 says & I quote, *"And when he saw their faith, he said unto him, man, thy sins are forgiven thee."* Luke 7:50 says & I quote, *"And he said to the woman, thy faith hath saved thee; go in peace."* Faith gives one the ability to do great wonders & signs! Acts 6:8 says & I quote, *"And Stephen, full of faith and power, did great wonders and miracles among the people."* Faith enables addition & multiplication! Acts 11:24 says & I quote, *"For he was a good man & full of the Holy Ghost and of faith and much people was added unto the Lord."* Through your own faith, rapid progress shall be mapped! You shall never lack for your faith shall be your provision!

APRIL EDITION

Theme: Being Planted
In The Lord's House
(Psalm 92:12-14)

25th Day

"The righteous will flourish like a palm tree, they will grow like a cedar of Lebanon; planted in the house of the LORD, they will flourish in the courts of our God. They will still bear fruit in old age, they'll stay fresh & green."

> ## PROGRESS CONFESSION:
>
> *I'm destined to flourish in & out of season! I've the anti-aging anointing! I'm never going to grow old but I'm going to stay fresh & green! I'm youthful forever!*

If you really want to grow & flourish well in this life, the equation is simple; just make sure you are planted in the house of the Lord. You have to be planted (rooted) in the house of the Lord the way a palm tree is planted (rooted) in the ground. Being planted in the Lord means that all your provision will be coming from the Lord Himself. Psalm 37:25 says & I quote, *"I've been young, and now am old; yet have I not seen the righteous forsaken, nor his seed begging bread."* What is it that is found in the house of God? In the house of the Lord, there is silver & gold! 2 Kings 16:8 says & I quote, *"And Ahaz took the silver and gold that was found in the house of the Lord & in the treasures of the king's house & sent it for a present to the king of Assyria."* In the house of the Lord, there is money! 2 Kings 12:10 says & I quote, *"And it was so, when they saw that there was much money in the chest, that the king's scribe and the high priest came up, & they put up in bags, & told the money that was found in the house of the Lord."* In the house of the Lord, there are rooms (houses)! 2 Chronicles 31:11 says & I quote, *"Then Hezekiah commanded to prepare chambers in the house of the Lord; and they prepared them."* As you will be dwelling in the house of the Lord, goodness & mercy shall follow you all the days of your life (Psalm 23:6). Psalm 27:4 says & I quote, *"One thing have I desired of the Lord, that will I seek after; that I may dwell in the house of the Lord all the days of my life, to behold the beauty of the Lord, & to enquire in his temple."* As you will be in the house of the Lord, the beauty of the Lord will be being bestowed upon you! Excellence shall be your portion! In your old age, you shall be able to bear good fruits! Fresh, pure, green & good fruits are your portion! You shall never lack anything!

APRIL EDITION

Theme: Mastering
Your Strengths
(Psalm 84:7)

26th Day

"They go from strength to strength, every one of them in Zion appeareth before God."

> ## PROGRESS CONFESSION:
> I'm strong! I'm stronger! From strength to strength, I'm moving stronger & mightier! The Lord is my strength in & out of season! I will never be weary!

Isaiah 40:29-31 says & I quote, *"He giveth power to the faint & to them that have no might he increaseth strength. Even the youths shall faint & be weary & the young men shall utterly fall: but they that wait upon the Lord shall renew their strength; they shall mount up with wings as eagles; they shall run & not be weary & they shall walk & not faint."* The Lord is about to give you power where you have been weak! The Lord is about to increase your strength where you had no mightiness before! Where others will be fainting, getting weary & utterly falling, your strength is going to be renewed! Where others will be incurring losses, you shall mount up your wings (sales, revenue & income, retaining huge volumes, greater & unimaginable profits) like eagles (great corporates that control the economy). You shall do business & do business but you shall never get weary nor faint! Your business (company) is going to be always on the flourishing side! You are going to move from strength to strength! You are going to open new branches & new niches! Lack shall be a thing of the past! Long life is your portion! Prosperity is your daily bread! Riches & wealth are your inheritance from the Lord! Freedom is your portion! Nothing shall by any means hurt nor distract you! Luke 10:19 says & I quote, *"Behold, I give unto you power to tread on serpents & scorpions & over all the power of the enemy & nothing shall by any means hurt you."* Philippians 4:13 says & I quote, *"I can do all things through Christ which strengtheneth me."*

<u>APRIL EDITION</u>

Theme: A Sound Mind
(2 Timothy 1:7)

27th Day

*"For God hath not given us the spirit of fear; but of power,
and of love, and of a sound mind."*

PROGRESS CONFESSION:

*My mind is renewed! I have a sound mind now! I have
the spirit of power, of love & of a sound mind! I fear
nothing for I have power & authority!*

As a
believer in Christ (a new creature), you are bound by the new lifestyle
principles to have the renewal of the mind for this will help you to adapt
fast to the new environment, welfare & warfare, so as to manoeuvre well.
Romans 12:1-3 says & I quote, *"I beseech you therefore, brethren, by the mercies
of God, that ye present your bodies a living sacrifice, holy, acceptable unto God, which
is your reasonable service. And be not conformed to this world: but be ye transformed
by the renewing of your mind, that ye may prove what is that good & acceptable &
perfect, will of God. For I say, through the grace given unto me, to every man that
is among you, not to think of himself more highly than he ought to think; but to
think soberly, according as God hath dealt to every man the measure of faith."* This
renewal of the mind will help you get to know, understand & prove (live
& or do business) a lifestyle that is good, acceptable & in the perfect
will of God. Learn to be considerate, for whatever we are to do in this
life is all according to the measure of faith God has granted to us. Think
soberly about others & yourself as well! Proverbs 23:7 says & I quote,
*"For as he thinketh in his heart, so is he: Eat & drink, saith he to thee; but his heart
is not with thee."* Fear nothing, for you have been given both power & the
spirit of power! The spirit of power is the one that gives one authority &
power! Luke 10:19 says & I quote, *"Behold, I give unto you power to tread on
serpents & scorpions, & over all the power of the enemy & nothing shall by any means
hurt you."* Fear not, the Lord is going to help you (Isaiah 41:13)! Isaiah
41:10 says & I quote, *"Fear thou not; for I'm with thee: be not dismayed; for I'm
thy God: I'll strengthen thee; yea, I'll help thee; yea, I'll uphold thee with the right
hand of my righteousness."* Joel 2:21-22 says & I quote, *"Fear not, O land; be
glad & rejoice: for the Lord will do great things. Be not afraid, ye beasts of the field:*

for the pastures of the wilderness do spring, for the tree beareth her fruit, the fig tree & *the vine do yield their strength."* You shall lack nothing! You are blessed! You are loved! You have love! You are an awesome person that was uniquely, fearfully & wonderfully made (Psalm 139:14) in God's image & after His likeness (Genesis 1:26) so as to be fruitful, multiply, fill the earth, subdue earth (kingdoms) & have dominion (Genesis 1:28) through a sound mind!

APRIL EDITION

Theme: Being Doers
of The Word of God
(James 1:22)

28th Day

*"But be ye doers of the word, and not hearers only,
deceiving your own selves."*

PROGRESS CONFESSION:

I'm going to be a doer of the Word of God in & out of season! My life is blessed in & out of season! I don't struggle to get money & make notable progress!

For progress to be progress, action has to be effective. You have to be doers of the Word of God not just simply hearers. Progress needs one to implement that which he or she is to hear, learn & or discover from the Word of God. Be a doer & not just a hearer! Do not deceive yourself by not doing that which the Word prescribes you to for the word of God is like medicine. Doing that which the Word prescribes you to do, makes your heart to merry (joyful). Proverbs 17:22 says & I quote, *"A merry heart doeth good like a medicine: but a broken spirit drieth the bones."* Joshua 1:7-8 says & I quote, *"Only be thou strong & very courageous, that thou mayest observe to do according to all the law, which Moses my servant commanded thee: turn not from it to the right hand or to the left, that thou mayest prosper withersoever thou goest. This book of the law shall not depart out of thy mouth; but thou shalt meditate therein day & night, that thou mayest observe to do according to all that is written therein: for then thou shalt make thy way prosperous and then thou shalt have good success."* Be strong & courageous so that you may be able to observe that which the Word entails us to do for us to be prosperous. Progress, prosperity & good success are all results of day & night meditation. Being a doer of the Word brings justification (Romans 2:13)! Being a doer of the Word brings the blessing of the Lord! James 1:23-25 says & I quote, *"For if any be a hearer of the word & not a doer, he is like unto a man beholding his natural face in a glass: for he behold himself & goeth his way & straightway forgeteth what manner of man he was. But whoso looketh into the perfect law of liberty & continueth therein, he being not a forgetful hearer, but a doer of the work, this man shall be blessed in his deed."* Proverbs 10:22 says & I quote, *"The blessing of the Lord, it maketh rich & he addeth no sorrow with it."*

APRIL EDITION

Theme: The Power
To Get Wealth
(Deuteronomy 8:18)

29th Day

"But thou shalt remember the Lord thy God: for it is he that giveth thee power to get wealth, that he may establish his covenant which he sware unto thy fathers, as it is this day."

> ## PROGRESS CONFESSION:
> *I'm not weak but I'm strong physically, economically, academically, socially, spiritually & or financially for the Lord is my inspiration, salvation, strength &*

Wealth is not just gotten by any Tom & Jerry, but it is gotten by those that have well understood that wealth is gotten through the God-given power. Wealth comes as result of the establishment of the covenants which the Lord would have sworn already unto our fathers. Once God has given you His glory, power & authority; wealth is going to be attracted to you for wealth is not worked for but you simply get it as a result of God's glory, wisdom, power & authority in you (Ecclesiastes 5:19). Solomon never worked for his riches & wealth but he asked for the power to get wealth (thus, God's glory, wisdom, power & authority to rule his people well). Wisdom, knowledge, power, glory & authority from above are all like magnet, they attract wealth to themselves. 2 Chronicles 1:12 says & I quote, *"Wisdom & knowledge is granted unto thee & I'll give thee riches & wealth & honour, such as none of the kings have had that have been before thee, neither shall there any after thee have the like."* So if you want really wealth, then ask for the *power (Deuteronomy 8:18), glory (Proverbs 25:2), wisdom (Proverbs 4:7), knowledge (Daniel 11:32) & authority (Luke 10:19) of God* that is accompanied by wealth accumulation. Seek yea first His kingdom (power) & all these things shall be added unto you (Matthew 6:33). Once you get the wealth, just put it in your mind that that wealth is not there for you to show off but rather it's there as your daily defence. Ecclesiastes 7:12 says & I quote, *"For wisdom is a defence & money is a defence: but the excellency of knowledge is, that wisdom giveth life to them that have it."* Proverbs 18:11 says & I quote, *"The rich man's wealth is his strong city, & as an high wall in his own conceit."*

APRIL EDITION

Theme: Taking Delight
In The Lord
(Psalm 37:4)

30th Day

"Take delight in the Lord & He'll give you the desires of your heart."

> ## PROGRESS CONFESSION:
> *I have taken delight in the Lord & the desires of my heart are about to be given to me! In Him, I will forever trust & truly rely! In Him, I'm confident, safe,*

Proverbs 16:3 says & I quote, ***"Commit to the LORD whatever you do, and He will establish your plans."*** We may plan all we may want, but real establishment comes from the Lord for He has already set plans for us (Jeremiah 29:11). 2 Chronicles 20:20 says & I quote, ***"And they rose early in the morning & went forth into the wilderness of Tekoa and as they went forth, Jehoshaphat stood & said, hear me, O Judah & ye inhabitants of Jerusalem; believe in the Lord your God, so shall ye be established; believe his prophets, so shall ye prosper."*** If you are desiring to be established be it; in marriage, business, profession, trade, company, industry etc., commit your works unto the Lord, have delight Him & then be ready & expectant to see the establishment manifold as the Lord will be giving you the desires of your heart. I prophesy in the name of Jesus Christ that as we ending April today, may it be the end of your dryness season be it; socially, mentally, academically, physically, spiritually, economically, politically & or financially! Doors that have been closed are opening on their own now & your duty is to only walk in! Walk in into your miracle marriage & or relationship! Walk into your financial freedom & or breakthrough! Walk into your company, niche & or business! Walk into your supernatural provision! Walk into your destiny helpers! Psalm 37:23-25 says & I quote, ***"The steps of a good man are ordered by the Lord & he delight in his way. Though he fall, he shall not be utterly cast down: for the Lord uphold him with his hand. I've been young & now am old; yet have I not seen the righteous forsaken, nor his seed begging bread."***

APRIL EDITION

Victory Prayer

Dear Lord, God of Abraham, Isaac & Jacob, I pray today that may you kindly pour out upon my family & I, a full amount of grace, favour & blessings that was upon our father of faith Abraham's life & family. O Lord, release the greater grace for wealth & anti-aging anointing into our lives & allow us live long for your glory & praise. May the Deborah's bravery & finishing anointing be upon our lives for us to live victorious lives. Help us, O Lord to live decent, holy, graceful, healthy, peaceful, organized, blessed, perfect & prosperous lives according to thy will. You've given us the assurance (through your cross & resurrection) that with you nothing is impossible. O Lord, establish your Word in us & let us all live in its full manifestation. Thank you, O Lord, for you always answer our prayers in the name of Jesus Christ, amen. ***Congratulations*Amphlope*Makorokoto***

APRIL EDITION

Salvation Call

Scripture: Romans 10:13 "For whoever calls on the name of the Lord shall be saved".

Prayer: Thank you, Lord, Jesus Christ for your Word which says that whosoever believes in your word & calls upon your name shall be saved. I therefore, come to you today confessing that I'm a sinner. May you forgive me all my sins. I believe in you, O Lord Jesus Christ that you died for my sins on the cross & on the third day you rose up from the dead full of power, life, grace & glory. O Lord, Jesus Christ, come into my heart, be my Lord & my Saviour. Lead me & guide me in all my errands from today onwards. I'm now yours, take control of me. Thank you, O Lord for saving my soul. I've eternal life now in the name of Jesus Christ, amen.

APRIL EDITION

Contact Details

Charity Monday Publishers
t/a CM Publishers
4009 Ebenezer, Southgate, Harare South
Mobile: +263774571035/
+263737183626
www.facebook.com/cmpublishers[1]
Linkedin Account: Mukaro Matuhwa
Facebook Account: Mkaro Mathwa
Email: tmmatuhwa@gmail.com
Instagram: @mmathwa

---

1. http://www.facebook.com/cmpublishers

T is a devotional booklet that was written by Mukaro Matuhwa who was born & bred in Masvingo. Mukaro Matuhwa did his elementary primary education at Mbuyanehanda Primary School, his secondary education at Silveira High School & his tertiary education at Harare Institute of Technology. He is eyeing to be a global author, acme engineer, seasoned believer and a chartered accountant. APRIL: Month of Rapid Progress is a 1 Tinothy 4:15 as based booklet that I've written containing 30 rapid progress teachings that are in a progressive way such that any believer who is eager to live a better lifestyle in this new month of April can easily follow for his or her own beneficiation. Progress is bound to be evident the moment you are to start applying progress-based principles. Applied principles gives birth to undeniable progress evidence in everything that concerns you; be it social life, business life, ministry, finances, health etc. Be ready to embrace a shift in your life as you'll be going through the pages of this devotional booklet in this month of April which has been declared to be the month of Rapid Progress. Rapid progress is your portion! God bless you.